Ethnic Conflicts in Schools

Ethnic Conflicts in Schools

Susan Banfield

—Multicultural Issues—

ENSLOW PUBLISHERS, INC.

44 Fadem Road   P.O. Box 38
Box 699   Aldershot
Springfield, N.J. 07081   Hants GU12 6BP
U.S.A.   U.K.

Library of Congress Cataloging-in-Publication Data

Banfield, Susan
    Ethnic Conflits in Schools / Susan Banfield.
        p. cm. — (Multicultural Issues)
    Includes bibliographical references (p.) and index.
    ISBN 0-89490-640-2
    1. Discrimination in education–United States–Juvenile literature. 2. Minority
students–Crimes against–United States–Juvenile literature. 3. Ethnic relations–Juvenile
literature. 4. School violence–United States–Juvenile literature. 5. Conflict
management–United States–Juvenile literature. [1. Ethnic relations. 2. School violence.
3. Prejudices.] I. Title II. Series.
LC212.2.B35 1995   94-34359
371.5'8–dc20   CIP
                                                 AC
Printed in the United States of America

10 9 8 7 6 5 4 3 2 1

Photo Credits: Lawrence Elementary School, Tucson, AZ, p. 51; Matthew
Heffernan, pp. 37, 82; Michael Kesselman, Ph.D. pp. 72, 76, 91; Museum of the City
of New York, p. 10; UPI / Bettman, pp. 27, 58; UPI / Bettman / Pete Harris, p. 20.

Cover Photo: AP / Wide World Photos.

Contents

chapter

1

A Case History

A Portuguese-American teenager at a San Jose, California high school had learned how to make obscene remarks in Vietnamese from the movie *Born on the Fourth of July*. One day, with friends around to support him, he started taunting a group of Vietnamese-American students at his school with his new vocabulary.

The Vietnamese-American students were deeply outraged and called on friends from another school for help. Two days later, a group of about a dozen Vietnamese-American students drove up to the high school, got out of their cars, and began arguing with a group of white youths who were gathered on a sidewalk taking their morning break. Suddenly, one of the Vietnamese-American youths pulled out a gun. He fired a warning shot, then began firing at random.

Most of the students in the area screamed and fled in panic. One fifteen-year-old white boy, not put off by the warning shot, kept coming forward. His only thought was to try to help settle the dispute. The Vietnamese-American boy with the gun shot and fatally wounded him. He died at a local hospital several hours later. This incident, which happened in May of 1990 is more tragic than most that are associated with ethnic conflicts in schools—but it is far from unique. In this book, ethnic conflict is defined as conflict of any kind, from simple tension to physical fights, that arises between members of different ethnic groups, mainly *because of* their cultural and/or racial differences.

The high school at which this disaster occurred is ethnically mixed: 39 percent Hispanic American, 21 percent Anglo American, 28 percent Asian American and Pacific Islander, 11 percent African American, and 1 percent Native American. The school had a history of ethnic tension and of gangs. The two problems are closely related. According to the school's director of Intergroup Relations, gangs are often formed out of a need an ethnic group will feel to defend itself against being picked on by other groups. Despite the tensions and the presence of gangs, the school had experienced relatively little violence. It was aware of its problems and had been taking action. It was especially serious about cracking down on gangs and had banned all gang-related clothing, such as the red and blue neckerchiefs gang members called "rags."

None of those involved in the shooting were evil or nasty. The killer himself was described by a psychologist as a bright but naive teenager who got caught up in a violent situation and got scared.[1] Still, the tragedy happened.

Immediately following the incident, students themselves took actions to try to heal the wounds. Although the attack did not appear to be gang-related, at least fifteen students at the victim's high school who were gang members took off their "colors" (clothing that carries the name and/or insignia of a specific gang) and publicly announced that they were leaving their gangs.

Teachers and administrators also took action. They made plans to start a support group for Vietnamese-American students. They put more emphasis in their classes and after-school activities on appreciating and understanding other cultures. New rules assured that all ethnic groups would be represented on the student council. A special large assembly was held to encourage appreciation of the school's diverse student body.

The next fall, the student body president declared that the school no longer had any real ethnic conflict, that it was time to move on.

Yet things did not remain quiet. Two years after the shooting, white parents in the neighborhood began a campaign to reopen the case and bring new charges against the boy who had killed "one of their own." The Vietnamese-American teen had already pleaded guilty to a charge of first degree murder and been locked up for it. Now the parents wanted him convicted of having committed a hate crime as well. (A hate crime is one that is motivated by prejudice against members of a particular racial, ethnic, or religious group.) The group's efforts were not successful. But they

The students shown here saluting the flag were attending the Mott Street Industrial School in New York City in 1889-1890.

show how persistent the problem of ethnic conflict in a school can be. Even when a school population has been made keenly aware that it must deal forcefully with the problem, and even when both students and teachers have worked to bring peace to their school, tensions can still erupt.

Our nation's public schools are among the places where members of the country's dozens of different ethnic and racial groups are brought together and required to work together most closely. The problem of tensions between different ethnic groups has plagued American schools for years. The above story is about Anglos and Asians. Nearly identical stories could be told about African-American and Jewish students, or about Native-American and Anglo students. They can be told about rural and suburban schools as well as about inner-city schools.

Why are there tensions between the different ethnic and racial groups in our schools? A racial group is a group of people who share certain physical traits and often share a common history and culture as well. An ethnic group is one whose members are bound together by a shared history, culture, nationality, or religion. What can we do to prevent tragedies such as the one that struck this San Jose high school from ever happening? What, if anything, can we do to bring permanent peace to our schools? Will prejudice in schools ever be a thing of the past? These are the questions this book will attempt to answer.

A Long History

From its earliest beginnings, the United States has been a nation of immigrants from many lands. That is, a nation which is made up of people who have left their homes in other countries to come and make a new home here. Even before we were a nation, the colonies that would become the United States were populated by Dutch, German, Swedish, Irish, French, and English settlers. In the 1840s, millions of Irish came to this country to escape a potato famine. Potatoes were the main food in the Irish diet. In 1845 and 1846, a disease struck the potatoes and they rotted in the field. Conditions in Ireland were so bad that one million people died of starvation between 1845 and 1849. As many as could, left Ireland for the United States and other countries. Also in the 1800s, thousands of Chinese arrived on the West Coast of the United States hoping to help build the transcontinental railroad, the first railroad to stretch from the West Coast of the United States to the East Coast. Mexicans continued to settle in the territories of the Southwest (where they had been settling since the 1600s). Then, in the first two decades of the twentieth century, this country saw over ten million immigrants from southern and eastern Europe arrive at its doorstep, hoping to find a better life for themselves and their families. One of the things that attracted many people to the United States was the prospect of a free education for their children. And so, the children of most new immigrants entered the nation's public schools.

What was the result? Were schools of a century ago plagued by problems of ethnic conflict and tension?

Prejudice has been defined as "a judgment based on previous decisions formed before the facts were known."[1] Prejudice against foreigners has long been common in this country. Most immigrant groups faced fierce prejudice. There was even a time when an entire political party, the "Know Nothings," had a unifying theme of hatred of foreigners. In the 1800s this hostility was not often a big problem in schools because many immigrants were educated separately. The Irish and other Roman Catholic immigrants often organized parochial, in this case, Catholic, schools for their children. In other cases, the public system often provided separate schools. In the Southwest, Hispanic-American children were often made to attend separate schools.[2] Separate schools were operated for Asian-American children in California. An editorial in a San Francisco paper of the time read:

Our children should not be placed in any position where their youthful impressions may be affected by association with pupils of the Mongolian race.[3]

This was the era when the Supreme Court of the United States decided, in the case of *Plessy* v. *Ferguson,* that "separate but equal" schools were all right for black children. Tensions in schools might not have been an issue at this time. But this was not because people were any less prejudiced. It was simply due to the fact that schoolchildren of different ethnic and racial groups were often kept apart.

In the early 1900s, a number of educators had begun to have new and idealistic notions of what the mission of the nation's public schools should be. These progressive teachers and principals saw the schools as agents that could help solve social, economic, and political problems, as well as educate children. They also, for the first time, saw it as the job of the schools to help new immigrants to adjust to and become a part of mainstream American culture.

It was New York City that received the greatest number of new immigrants; its school population nearly doubled in the first fifteen years of this century.[4] New York City Superintendent William Henry Maxwell viewed his schools as a ladder "from the gutter to the university." He believed that education could and should help immigrant children to overcome all the many obstacles and inequalities they would face.[5] To that end he began many new programs designed to meet the needs of immigrant children. First, he ran many schools on double sessions, so that there would be a place in the public schools for every child who wanted to attend. It was Maxwell who introduced vocational and technical education to New York City schools, offering courses at night, for teens who had to work, as well as by day. He started special classes for students who did not yet speak English. Special classes were also offered for average students, students with learning disabilities, deaf students, blind students, and students with physical disabilities. He began many new after-school recreational and social programs.[6] Clearly Maxwell had tremendous compassion and respect for the city's foreign-born students and for their families.

Teachers who shared Maxwell's progressive and generous views were able to provide a respectful, encouraging, and understanding learning environment for all their students, no matter what their background. Unfortunately, there was often a large gap between the ideals of progressive educators and actual practices in many classrooms. Many teachers were far from patient with immigrant children. Many teachers were of Irish or German heritage and shared the deep prejudice against the new immigrants that was still the norm at that time.[7] Stereotypes about the new immigrant groups developed quickly and were used against their children in school. When immigrant children did poorly in school, this was used to confirm people's fears.[8] In 1896 a *New York Tribune* writer revealed an attitude typical of the time when he declared that public school teachers "have to deal largely with pupils who are offensively dirty and densely ignorant, both by inheritance and by force of circumstance."[9]

One reason the prejudice may have caused less friction in the early years of this century, however, was that schools were quite often homogeneous, that is, most of the children in any one school shared a common background. Immigrants tended to settle with their own, and neighborhood schools could easily become dominated by a single group. In New York City, a 1905 study revealed that an entire district in the school system was 94.5 percent Jewish.[10] The Jewish parents liked the segregation as much as anyone. They feared their children would meet with hostility if they went to school in a less heavily Jewish populated environment. In fact, parents protested fiercely when the city proposed transferring a number of Jewish children out of their original district to another district on the West Side.[11]

The great wave of immigration that marked the first two decades of the century ended with the introduction of immigrant quotas in 1924. The men, women, and children who came over during previous years adjusted to mainstream American society relatively quickly, largely due to the booming economy which made it easier for people to establish good lives for their families.[12] Obvious prejudice and tension around European immigrants subsided. However, in the years following World War II, an ethnic conflict of another sort was slowly beginning to build, a conflict which would throw American schools into turmoil that would last for decades. This was the conflict between white and black Americans.

The events of the Second World War and the years immediately following set the stage for change. Americans had been horrified by the racism of the Nazis, who had killed millions of Jews simply because they belonged to an ethnic group the Nazis thought was inferior. Black American involvement in the war had shown that blacks could perform equally with whites and that blacks and whites could work closely together. American blacks were also inspired by the successful stands against white colonialism that African blacks made in many nations in the early postwar years. In 1944 Gunnar Myrdal published *An American Dilemma: The Negro Problem and Modern Democracy.* This widely read exposé showed Americans the injustice of their legally segregated public life.

In the late 1940s and early 1950s, dozens of black communities challenged the notion of segregated education in the United States. They took their complaints to the courts. Finally, in 1952, one case, *Brown v. Topeka (Kansas) Board of Education,* made it to the United States Supreme Court. The Court's landmark decision was handed down May 17, 1954:

> *Does segregation of children in public schools solely on the basis of race, even though the physical facilities and other tangible factors may be equal, deprive the children of the minority group of equal educational opportunities? We believe that it does. . . . We conclude that in the field of public education, the doctrine of separate but equal has no place. Separate educational facilities are inherently unequal. . . .*[13]

Legally segregated schools would, from that point on, be

unconstitutional. A year later, on May 31, 1955, the Supreme Court ordered schools to desegregate, that is to allow blacks and whites to attend the same schools. Compliance with (obedience to) the order would require tremendous changes in many southern school systems. Because of this, no date was given for completion of the process of desegregation. Schools were only required to show a "prompt and reasonable start toward full compliance."[14]

On September 4, 1957, a small group of eight teenagers made their way slowly up the rise to Central High School in Little Rock, Arkansas. For simply a day at school, they were especially well dressed, the boys in suits and ties, the girls in neatly pressed skirts and blouses. They did not act in the carefree, spirited way students often do when returning from summer vacation. In fact, their faces were solemn, their eyes set straight ahead.

This was no ordinary group of friends, and this was no ordinary first day of school. The eight teens, joined at the top of the rise by a ninth, Elizabeth Eckford, were the first black students to attempt to enroll at formerly all-white Central High School. The city of Little Rock had decided to allow a handful of "qualified" black students to enroll at Central in order to carry out the recent federal decision requiring schools to desegregate.

The state's governor, Orval Faubus, had other ideas, however. The year before, Faubus had run for governor on the promise that he would never allow integration in the state of Arkansas. On the eve of Central High's opening day, Faubus

Elizabeth Eckford, one of the nine black students who attempted to enter Little Rock, Arkansas's all-white Central High School is shown surrounded by reporters after she and others were barred from entering the school by the Arkansas National Guard.

ordered the National Guard into Little Rock. He went on television to explain that he had taken this action to prevent violence. In fact, there was no evidence that there might be violence. The Guardsmen would be used to prevent the nine black students from entering the high school.

The three boys and six girls had been carefully coached by Daisy Bates, the wife of an editor of a local paper run by and published for blacks. Mrs. Bates had told them to be prepared to be insulted and to keep their dignity if anyone called them names. The coaching was more than put to the test. An all-white crowd had been gathering along the streets near Central High since 6 A.M. Some carried abusive signs. Others shouted obscenities and jeered at the students as they walked by. Elizabeth Eckford cried.[15] Then, when that seemingly endless walk up the short block to school finally ended, they were face to face with stern-faced National Guardsmen who, with their bayonets glistening in the sun, refused to let the students enter.

It took President Eisenhower calling in the 101st Airborne Division of the United States Army before the nine black teens at last made it inside the school. On September 23, seasoned paratroopers gave the students a military escort through the crowds and the taunts, and they entered Central High School.

The first months of desegregation at Little Rock's Central High School may have been more highly publicized than most. But the level of tension involved was typical. All over the South, tensions in schools reached all-time highs as systems began warily to comply with the Supreme Court order.

In the years following, tensions eased considerably. In some cases, such as that of Louisville, Kentucky, this was because the desegregation process went relatively smoothly. By the end of 1957, Louisville's schools had been completely—and voluntarily—desegregated.[16] In many places, however, this lack of tension was not because desegregation was going so unexpectedly well. It was because many school systems were taking advantage of the looseness of the terms in the Supreme Court order. The term "desegregated" was taken to mean admitting one or two blacks to an otherwise all-white school. The vagueness of the clause "prompt and reasonable start" was also taken advantage of. Many schools used it as an excuse to postpone taking action.

As a result, by the early 1960s only the bare beginnings of desegregation had been achieved in many parts of the South. In Charlotte, North Carolina, for example, only eight black students had been assigned to white schools by 1960.[17] But this was not a situation black Americans—nor many white Americans—would stand for for long. As outraged citizens began to press for action, tensions in the schools were reaching new heights.

In the fall of 1964, Mrs. Darius Swann of Charlotte, who was black, asked for her child to be transferred to a desegregated school. Her request was refused. In January of the following year she, her husband, and twenty-four other parents with similar complaints filed suit. Between 1965 and 1969, more extensive desegregation was undertaken. But by 1969 fourteen thousand out of the twenty-four thousand black students in the Charlotte–Mecklenburg school system still attended all-black schools.[18] A new judge, James B. McMillan, decided this was not good enough. It was not, he felt, what the Supreme Court had in mind.[19] He ordered total desegregation of the system's schools by the fall of 1970. Whatever means were necessary to comply with the order should be employed. If that meant that children would have to be bused, then they should be bused. Thus began one of the most conflict-ridden periods in the history of our nation's schools, the era of the busing controversy.

From the outset, the policy of busing children to schools in neighborhoods other than their own in order to achieve racial balance aroused intense feelings. In Charlotte, Judge McMillan issued a court order in February 1970 requiring that students be bused. Thousands of parents came to meetings to protest his decision. Over nineteen thousand signed an anti-busing petition.[20] Compliance was delayed as the decision was appealed to the United States Supreme Court. The Court, however, in a 9-0 vote in April of 1971, upheld the constitutionality of Judge McMillan's order. The following fall, busing began in Charlotte.

The first year of busing was a year filled with fear, suspicion, violence, and anger. Blacks as well as whites were apprehensive. They often didn't want to go into a new school where they would be treated as second-class citizens and where positions of leadership would be closed to them.[21]

Fighting was common that first year. Many students, to escape as much of the tension and conflict as they could, stopped participating in extracurricular activities. A special information center was set up just to handle calls and complaints about busing.

After the Supreme Court's Charlotte–Mecklenburg decisions, the experience of Charlotte was duplicated in many other communities. In the 1970s there was violent unrest all over the country as buses carried black children into white schools in order to achieve full desegregation.

But the turmoil was not only to be found in the South. The Charlotte–Mecklenberg decision made it clear that *de facto* segregation would no longer be tolerated, wherever it occurred. The term "*de facto* segregation" describes situations in which blacks are not forced by law to attend all-black schools, but in which other circumstances ensure that schools are chiefly all-black or all-white. In fact, one of the most violent, turbulent experiences with busing in the country occurred in the northern city of Boston.

Boston had long been a city of clearly defined neighborhoods, some black, some white. Blacks were kept out of the white neighborhoods; landlords refused to rent to them. White neighborhoods had better city services, better housing, and significantly better schools. The school buildings themselves were in better shape. The teachers were better trained. Books were newer and up-to-date. There were more advanced courses and after-school activities. Boston's schools were set up on a neighborhood basis, with students required to attend the schools in their neighborhood. This meant that blacks were effectively denied access to white schools and their many advantages.

In the 1960s, encouraged by the civil rights activity in the South, blacks in Boston began to protest the *de facto* segregation in the city's schools. In 1965, Massachusetts passed the Racial Imbalance Act and became the first state to outlaw *de facto* segregation.

But sentiment against integrating, or bringing blacks and whites together in the schools, was strong in many neighborhoods. The Racial Imbalance Act had almost no effect. The city had a new open enrollment policy, which permitted students to transfer freely into any school in the system. Each year thousands of white students made use of open enrollment to transfer to new schools. But blacks who attempted to make use of the policy were prevented from doing so. Black parents were not told of available places in white schools, or their requests for transfers were denied. Those few black students who did manage to transfer into white schools often were forced to sit separately or were encouraged by guidance counselors to leave.[22] Finally, black parents decided to take the matter before the courts.

On June 21, 1974, Federal Judge W. Arthur Garrity, Jr., ruled:

> *The defendants have knowingly carried out a systematic program of segregation . . . and have intentionally maintained a dual school system. Therefore, the entire school system is unconstitutionally segregated.*[23]

Judge Garrity presented the school system with a plan which would result in full segregation by the end of the second year. The plan's chief means of achieving this goal was busing. Schools in black neighborhoods were paired with schools in white neighborhoods. Students from one school in the pair would be bused to the second school in the pair until racial balance was achieved.

The reaction of whites in one neighborhood was violent. They formed an organization called ROAR (Restore Our Alienated Rights) and held anti-busing rallies on twelve consecutive Sundays. On the opening day of school, hundreds of whites gathered outside South Boston High with tomatoes, bananas, beer cans, and rocks in hand to throw at the buses.[24] Once school had begun and the buses were rolling, violence occurred on a daily basis. Every day angry white crowds gathered near the schools, yelling out their protests. They threw stones at the buses and often shouted obscenities. Inside, fights were commonplace. A black junior high school student named Richie Wallace described his experience:

> *Every day we get off the bus and a crowd of white kids call us "nigger" and "bonehead." They threaten us and tell us, "Go back to Africa." Once, they sent little white kids with white sheets running through the school, saying "The Klansmen are coming!"*
>
> *The white teachers never explain the work to us. Sometimes they call us stupid. And they say we can't do the work. I don't think they care if we learn at all.[25]*

26

Police in Boston keep a crowd of whites back as a school bus carrying black students arrives at South Boston High School. Thousands of white schoolchildren in Boston refused to enter court-ordered desegregated schools on the first day of classes.

One major purpose of busing was to create a situation in which blacks and whites could learn to live together in harmony. Initially, it is clear, busing only brought schools further away from this goal. The racial tensions in Charlotte, Boston, and other communities reached all-time highs. But what about in the long run? Was busing worth it?

In Boston, it would be hard to answer "yes." Judge Garrity had to closely watch over the situation in his city for over a decade. During that time he issued 415 new orders to ensure that his original order was carried out. Although Boston's schools were completely desegregated by the end of two years, tensions between the races still exist today. Even the violence lasted, not tapering off until the 1980s. Also, as many as two thousand white children were withdrawn from the public schools and sent to newly opened segregated private schools. An untold number enrolled in the city's parochial schools. In all, about 10 percent of the system's students were lost to what is called "white flight."[26] Judges in other large cities, such as Dallas, Texas; Pasadena, California; Milwaukee, Wisconsin; and Louisville, Kentucky; were encouraged by what they saw in Boston to call for less strict busing plans.

Charlotte, on the other hand, had a very different experience. As early as spring of 1972—after only six months of busing—some people were already beginning to see benefits. The children were busing's earliest supporters and did much to bring around fearful and angry parents. Said one black parent:

28

> *They [the children] were our best sellers of busing. The anxieties that parents had disappeared when kids came home feeling pretty good about themselves and what had happened in school.*[27]

One white parent remarked:

> *"They gobbled up their breakfast and didn't want to be late. It was hard for the parent to counteract that."*[28]

Another white parent reported the same experience:

> *The change occurred when the child was eager to get on the bus and go to school. I know two parents who said their child made real good friends with a black child, and they didn't realize the child was black until halfway through the school year. There was a realization that the child didn't see any difference.*[29]

Many people changed their minds about busing after they had seen it working for a while. By 1978, students were once again participating in extracurricular activities and developing loyalties to their new, racially mixed schools. And by that point Charlotte was being looked to by other cities all over the country as proof that busing could work. Supporters said people simply had to give desegregation time.

So where does the truth lie? Most likely somewhere in the middle. Some systems share Charlotte's optimism. In Orangeburg, South Carolina, most whites who had left the public schools when the order for desegregation came down, eventually returned. Now the town's schools, close to half-black, half-white, have won national recognition for innovation and quality.[30] Other cities had bitter experiences of busing that were never set right. In Richmond, Virginia, busing left the schools nearly 90 percent black, with a large proportion of students coming from disadvantaged backgrounds. The white students who left during the "white flight" reaction to busing have never returned. Many middle class blacks have also left the system. Students and teachers report improved relations between black students and the white students who remain in the system. However, Richmond has had to struggle with serious problems of lowered academic performance among its many students.[31]

By the end of the 1970s, the era of racial tension that accompanied the integration of the nation's schools appeared to be coming to an end. In some cases this was because students and teachers had actually learned to live and work together more harmoniously. In other cases, unfortunately, it was because unsuccessful attempts at desegregation had left schools with largely unmixed populations. In any event, the country seemed to be weary of its decades-long struggle for racial equality and integration. The early 1980s were years of an uneasy truce in the nation's classrooms.

chapter 3

Schools Today

What is happening in our nation's schools?

•In New York City, two African-American children and one Hispanic-American child were attacked (in separate incidents) and their faces were stained with white paint.[1]

•In Chicago, African-American and Hispanic-American students recently engaged in gang warfare that injured thirteen students and one teacher and wound up with the arrests of sixty teens.[2]

•In Jacksonville, Florida, an all-white school yacht club rejected a minority student for membership, arousing strong feelings throughout the community.[3]

•In Dubuque, Iowa, in the heart of middle America, citizens recently made efforts to attract more black residents. This provoked a series of cross burnings and set off clashes between white and black students in the city's schools.[4]

The problem is as serious in the country's suburban and rural schools, as it is in big inner-city systems.

In the Boston suburb of Medford, Massachusetts, racial tensions erupted into a large fight in December of 1992 that involved over a hundred students. It took fifteen police officers using dogs and clubs to restore order. School was closed for a week afterwards.[5]

The public concern with civil rights that had dominated the United States for over twenty years seemed to have died down by the 1980s. But this was not because the nation's problems with prejudice had been solved. One observer noted that by 1986 "legal segregation [had] been almost universally replaced by *de facto* segregation in public schools, and in both South and North, most black and white school children [were] as 'separate' as in 1954, *if not more so.*"[6]

In the late 1980s, a *Time* magazine poll showed that 92 percent of black Americans and 87 percent of white Americans believed that "racial prejudice [was] still common in America."[7] In fact, not long after the civil rights movement wound down, problems with racial and ethnic prejudice began to increase again. The United States Department of Justice's Community Relations Service estimated that between the years 1980 and 1986, cases of racially motivated violence in the country had tripled.[8]

Has that trend continued into the 1990s? Some people say yes; others, no. Some studies show that people seem to be rejecting old ethnic stereotypes. For example, an organization called People for the American Way conducted a survey of

American young people between the ages of fifteen and twenty-four. The results gave an optimistic outlook on the state of relationships between members of different racial and ethnic groups. Over 70 percent of the young people surveyed had a close personal friend who was of another race. The majority of those surveyed saw themselves as much more comfortable than their parents in their interactions with people of other races. They also thought that even though improvement in relations between the races was happening slowly, there was definite improvement.[9]

However, other studies show that people today have prejudices that are more intense than in earlier years and that they are less likely than before to feel guilty about such attitudes. Another major poll, conducted in 1990 by Louis Harris, gave a much more discouraging picture. This was a poll of high school students.

High School Poll

- Less than half of the young people surveyed would try to stop a racial incident if they saw one.
- Nearly a third said they would actually participate in such an incident.
- 17 percent said they would give it silent support.
- The majority of the students surveyed had seen or heard about racial confrontations that had overtones of violence.[10]

Unfortunately, the statistics seem to show that the more negative picture of contemporary attitudes is the correct one—especially in our schools. An organization called Klanwatch, established by the Southern Poverty Law Center, surveys the news across the nation to keep track of hate crimes. Klanwatch has discovered that:

- Most hate crimes are committed by young people age twenty-five or under.[11]

- More than half of all hate crimes are committed by teens eighteen or under.[12]

- More and more of these are taking place at schools.

- In the first five months of 1992, there was a four-fold increase in the number of hate crimes committed at schools, as compared with the same period in 1991.[13]

"There are incidents occurring daily in the public schools," says Howard J. Ehrlich, director of research for the National Institute Against Prejudice and Violence.[14] U.S. Department of Education figures show a dramatic increase in complaints about ethnic or racial harassment in both the elementary and secondary schools.[15] The Los Angeles County School District alone has records of over twenty-two hundred reports of hate crimes in one school year (1989–1990).[16] Mr. Ehrlich's organization estimates that between 20 and 25 percent of students are the victims of racial or ethnic incidents every school year.[17]

However, these numbers may not even give the full

picture. Many incidents occur that, for one reason or another, never make it into the statistics. Danny Welch, the director of Klanwatch, points out that "we're only seeing a fraction of the actual incidents. Most hate crimes on school campuses are never reported to the police."[18] Another reason that the truth may be even worse than the numbers show is that people don't always realize that prejudice is involved in the incidents that occur at schools. Says Ronald Stephens, executive director of the National School Safety Center: "A far greater amount of school crime and violence is racially related than anyone wants to admit."[19]

What Forms Does Conflict Take?

Clearly, racial and ethnic tension is a problem still very much present in our nation's schools. Ethnic tensions can take many forms. Incidents of actual violence are the most obvious and dramatic signs that tensions are present, but prejudice and ethnic tension show themselves in many ways.

Name-calling. One common way students show their prejudice and promote racial or ethnic conflict is by name-calling. Hateful names exist for members of every racial or ethnic group. Students often learn these at a very young age from parents or older youths. Sometimes a simple tone of voice, or the mere fact that a member of another ethnic group is using a particular word, can turn a name into a racial slur. The neutral label "Jew" is often converted into a term of hate by non-Jewish speakers. Black students can get away with calling one another "nigger" when joking around together. But

35

coming from whites or anyone of another group, the word is one of pure hatred.

A recent national survey of school executives showed that there has been a dramatic rise in the general use of abusive language by students.[20] This has included a rise in the use of racial and ethnic slurs, insulting words directed at a person's race or ethnicity. In Orange County, California, black and white students started calling one another names after a white student won an air-guitar contest.[21] In Seattle, a crowd at a basketball game yelled "Miss it, nigger!" as a high school student attempted a free throw.[22] These are just a few of thousands of incidents that are reported.

Graffiti. Another common way for students to express prejudice and hate is through the use of graffiti. One of the attractions of graffiti is that it is a relatively safe way of expressing hatred anonymously and without much chance of getting caught. During the years of the busing controversies in Boston and Charlotte, graffiti was everywhere. There has been a rise in the use of racial graffiti in recent years. A number of schools have reported outbreaks of swastikas on school walls. The swastika was a symbol used by the Nazis, who persecuted the Jews during World War II, and ever since people have viewed it as a strong anti-Jewish symbol.

There has also been a dramatic increase in gang-related graffiti. Every gang has special identifying symbols. These symbols establish "turf." Gang-related graffiti helps to increase racial tensions. Gangs frequently set members of one racial or ethnic group against another. Tensions between gangs can

An upside down martini glass symbol, the same as those found in Poland following the Nazi invasion during World War II is shown here. The upside down glass means that "the party is over" for other gangs.

easily translate into tensions between racial groups. In many schools there is an aggressive anti-graffiti policy.

Hate mail. Still another way in which racial or ethnic prejudice is expressed is through hate mail or other hate publications. While not as common as name-calling or graffiti, hate publications can have a profoundly hurtful effect on those they are aimed at. Sometimes anonymous notes are sent to a particular person. In Palmetto, Georgia, for example, racist notes were left in the desk of an African-American elementary school student.[23] Other times, racist leaflets are distributed. In 1988, in a high school in Catawba County, North Carolina, flyers appeared that showed an African-American student hanging on a burning cross, a grave with a Jewish name on it, and various other Ku Klux Klan and Nazi symbols. The flyers called for the death of African-Americans and the rape of Jews.[24] The effect that such publications and letters have on the members of minority groups can be devastating.

Violence. Racial and ethnic tensions can also erupt in acts of physical violence. Violence in general is increasing in our nation's schools. The National Institute of Education reports that nearly 300,000 high school students are physically attacked every month. It is reported that at least one out of five high school students now carries a weapon.[25] A significant proportion of this violence is racially motivated.

Often, incidents of name-calling, graffiti, or hate mail can provoke physical violence. At Lenzinger High School in Lawndale, California, an African-American girl and a Hispanic-American girl began using racial slurs against each other. Soon they were fighting. Their fight increased tensions between African-American and Hispanic-American students generally at their school. By the end of the day, dozens of fights had broken out between African Americans and Hispanic Americans, and the police had to be called in.[26]

Another common source of tension that can easily escalate into violence is interracial dating. Fights have erupted over blacks dating whites in cities and towns from Ansonia, Connecticut, to Covington, Georgia.[27]

Sometimes violence seems to erupt for no reason at all. In Selma, Alabama, police uncovered a plot hatched by black students to randomly attack "white targets" around one of the city's middle schools. Thirty students were suspended after a series of assaults took place.[28] In Robeson County, North Carolina, two white teens shot a black high school student.[29]

The increase in gang activity has also accounted for some of the increase in racial and ethnic violence. Educators agree that gang involvement has been growing steadily. Now gangs are found in suburbs as well as in cities. Middle school as well as high school students are commonly involved,[30] and in some places even elementary school students are joining.[31] For gangs, fights and violence are a way of life. Some gangs are racially mixed, but others divide up sharply along racial lines.

Even at schools where incidents of name-calling, graffiti, or racial fights are rare or nonexistent, tension may still exist. Often it shows up in the cafeteria, where many schools report that students still segregate themselves by racial or ethnic group. Or it shows up around school social events, where

39

students of different groups cannot agree over music or, for other reasons, are reluctant to party together. Wherever there are differences and separation, there is an increase in tensions. As William Taylor, a member of a Washington, D.C. civil rights group called the Center for National Policy Review, noted, "Separation breeds fear and misunderstanding."[32] Fear and misunderstanding, in turn, make for tension and conflict.

Who Is Involved?

American public schools today are more diverse than ever. Urban schools frequently have students from dozens of different ethnic groups. Brooklyn, New York, counts 94 different groups.[33] Miami, Florida, has students from 147 countries.[34] By 1990, minority students accounted for more than 50 percent of the school population in California, Arizona, New Mexico, and Texas.[35] Suburban schools are also becoming more culturally mixed. Newton, Massachusetts, a suburb of Boston, was once overwhelmingly white. Now it has students from over sixty countries at one of its high schools.[36] Ethnic prejudice has been directed toward many of the groups who have recently entered our nation's schools. Often the members of the group that have arrived most recently are the targets.

To many people the terms "ethnic conflict" and "racial conflict" call to mind the country's age-old problems between blacks and whites. However, they can refer to conflicts between any number of different groups.

Hispanic Americans are one of this nation's largest

minorities. Prejudice against Hispanic Americans is long-standing and widespread. People are prejudiced against students of Mexican heritage in the West and Southwest, against Puerto Rican students in the East, against Cubans in Miami, and against students from a variety of other Latin and Central American countries throughout the United States. Some high schools in inner-city Los Angeles have student populations that are as much as 80 percent Hispanic-American. Yet almost all of the teachers are white.[37] There are major language and cultural barriers that get in the way of the two groups understanding one another. Tensions between students and their teachers in such situations are common. Many students feel that their teachers have prejudices toward Hispanic-American students and therefore underestimate their abilities. One Los Angeles high school reports that there is little violence between the Hispanic-American students and the white school staff. But there is a constant level of tension that lowers the quality of school life. Teachers tend to avoid contact with students outside of class, rush to the cafeteria during breaks, and leave quickly at the end of the day to beat the traffic home. Students remain aloof, seldom turning to their teachers when they have a problem.[38] Such situations are commonplace.

Jewish students also frequently feel the sting of prejudice. Prejudice against Jews is one of the oldest, most deep-seated prejudices in our culture. In recent years there has been an increase in anti-Jewish incidents at schools. Swastikas have become a common type of graffiti. Some students responsible for such graffiti may not be fully aware that swastikas were

41

used as symbols by the Nazis, who put to death more than six million Jews, making these symbols extremely offensive to those of the Jewish faith. But in other cases, those responsible are fully aware of the significance of what they are drawing. In either case, the appearance of the Nazi symbols on school property has stirred up old feelings and created a great deal of tension and conflict.

Chatham, New Jersey, is a largely white community with very few Jewish families. In preparation for a soccer match against Millburn, a nearby community which is heavily Jewish, a group of students in the Chatham Pep Club made a banner that showed two stick figures at the back of a train. (Most Pep Club banners featured a train, as "Chatham Choo Choo" was part of a well-known school cheer.) One figure in the banner, a girl, had gold rings on a stick. These were supposed to represent bagels, a type of bread that is part of Jewish culture. The other figure, a man, had long hair and wore a black coat and a top hat. He was supposed to be a Hasidic Jew. (Members of the Hasidic sect of Judaism have a distinctive, traditional manner of dress.) The banner clearly showed insensitivity and some degree of anti-Jewish prejudice on the part of the student who drew it. Its effects were devastating. Many who saw the banner and didn't know about the "Chatham Choo Choo" thought it represented Jews on a train bound for a concentration camp. Both Jews and non-Jews were outraged. The few Jewish students and teachers at Chatham High were very hurt and upset. It took a great effort on the part of the administration and the entire school community to make amends for the hurt feelings and to restore trust. The principal and teachers looked carefully at the content of their courses to be sure they promoted values of tolerance and understanding of different ethnic groups. A university professor who specialized in diversity in education came in to work with the teachers, students, and administration of the school, and many workshops were held. Committees of both parents and teachers were formed to promote respect for cultural diversity.[39]

In the southwest region of the country, there are frequently tensions between Native-American students and their white teachers and classmates. Native-American students frequently feel subtle rejection by whites.[40] There are significant differences between Native-American and white culture. The learning style of Native Americans tends to be visual rather than verbal.[41] There is much less emphasis on competition and individual recognition in Native-American culture than there is in mainstream American society. Those who are not aware of such differences are likely to judge Native-American students as slow or lazy. Native-American students are very sensitive to such negative judgments, no matter how subtly they are expressed. Even when non-Native Americans are not passing negative judgments, many frequently fail to see Native Americans as unique individuals and in subtle ways ignore or exclude them. Native-American children seldom respond to their feelings of being judged or ignored with aggression. Instead, they tend to be quiet and retreat. Friendships between Native-American students and whites are more rare than between other ethnic groups.[42] Many Native-American youngsters leave school altogether. The national drop-out rate among Native-American students is almost 30 percent.[43] Studies show that Native-American children have one of the poorest self-concepts of any ethnic group of the country.[44] In this case, ethnic tensions may lack the drama of violent forms of expression, yet in the long run can have an even more devastating effect.

Prejudice against Asian-American students (including Chinese, Japanese, Koreans, Southeast Asians, and Pacific Islanders) is in some ways similar to prejudice against Native Americans. It is often subtle, and while not openly hateful or hostile, can still have deeply hurtful effects. Asian-American students, like Native Americans, frequently find that others do not view them as individuals, or they find that they are excluded or ignored.

Asian-American students have traditionally excelled academically, more so than members of any other minority group. In 1985, 70 percent of Asian-American eighteen-year-olds took the SAT (a national college entrance exam). By contrast, only 28 percent of eighteen-year-olds in the country as a whole took the exam. Furthermore, the average math score of Asian-American seniors who took the test was forty-three points higher (out of a possible 800) than the national average.[45] Asian-American students' reputation for academic excellence has led to jealousy and resentment on the part of other students. This has fueled numerous conflicts. The United States Civil Rights Commission has pointed out that anti-Asian violence and harassment occurs regularly across the country.[46] The situation is particularly rough in inner-city schools. Asian students are frequently threatened and called "Chink" or "Chop Suey." One year, Washington Irving High School in New York City reported forty incidents of violence and harassment aimed at Asian-American students.[47]

The problem of ethnic conflicts in our schools is a serious and growing one. It involves students and teachers of many different racial and ethnic groups. It shows itself in many different ways. Seemingly minor conflicts can easily turn into major ones. Ethnic conflict in schools is a problem that needs to be addressed seriously. But before we can find solutions, we must first try to understand the causes.

4

The Causes
of Conflict

A friendship had developed between a Cambodian-American
student and an African-American student at a neighborhood
elementary school. One day the African-American student
shouted across the playground to her friend. The
Cambodian-American girl bowed her head and turned away. She
felt ashamed. In her culture, it was considered humiliating to be
singled out in a crowd. Her friend also felt hurt and embarrassed,
but for different reasons. The young African-American girl
thought her new friend had just rejected her.[1]

Incidents such as the above are common at schools where
the students have different backgrounds. In this case the misunderstanding did not lead to violence. In many cases,
however, this lack of awareness of the different values or practices of other cultural groups does lead to fighting, or at least
causes tensions. Misunderstandings about cultural traditions
are a common source of racial or ethnic conflict.

47

Prejudice. By far the largest cause of ethnic conflicts in schools, is prejudice. Racial or ethnic prejudice is a specific kind of prejudice, based on "faulty reasoning and inflexible generalizations" directed toward a specific group.[2] Racial prejudice consists of judgments made about the members of a particular group based on ideas about that group—usually negative—that have no clear connection to the individuals being judged. How do children become prejudiced? The most immediate reason is simply because their parents are. Much prejudice is learned.[3] This fact helps to explain the great difficulty our society has had in overcoming racial prejudice. If every night a child goes home to a house where he hears his parents talking in hateful terms about members of another group, the effect of any efforts at reducing prejudice will be minimal.

Some prejudice seems to arise naturally whenever people are confronted with others who seem strange or different. Studies show that the greater the physical differences between the members of two groups, the higher the incidence of prejudice between them.[4] For example, prejudice towards Native Americans seems to be less on the part of Hispanic-American students than it is on the part of white students.[5] This may in part be explained by the relationship mentioned above between prejudice and degree of difference. Hispanic Americans and Native Americans look more alike than do whites and Native Americans.

There are still other causes of prejudice. Many agree that the political climate of the time has an effect. In some eras, it is simply more acceptable to express prejudice than it is in others. The United States became progressively more conservative throughout the 1980s. That is, people turned away from the newer political attitudes of recent decades, especially from the belief that the government should strive to create economic equality for all people and should provide extra help for less fortunate members of society. During the 1980s, the Reagan administration reversed many gains that had been made in the area of civil rights in the previous two decades. In the late 1980s, for example, the federal government cut subsidized housing programs by 79 percent, training programs by 70 percent, the Work Incentive Program by 71 percent, and compensatory education programs for young children by 12 percent.[6] Attempts were made to undermine affirmative action programs. ("Affirmative action" describes efforts made to make up for the disadvantage minorities were at due to years of inferior treatment. These efforts consist largely of giving them preferential treatment in college admissions and job hiring.) And the government supported the apartheid (separatist) government in South Africa which enforced legal segregation of blacks and whites. This all helped to create a climate in which prejudice was able to breed. With the government displaying less concern for the welfare of minorities, people naturally felt freer to express hatreds of these groups.[7]

Another important factor in the recent rise of prejudice has been the economic decline the country has experienced. When jobs become scarce, and competition for them increases, people are more likely to resent members of other

49

ethnic groups, especially newly arrived immigrant groups. They believe these people are going to snatch rare job opportunities from them. Such beliefs may not be true. People going through hard times want to pin the blame for their difficulties on someone. Whether their views are well-founded or not, they still help to create prejudice and ethnic tensions. In city after city, school officials are quick to point out the relationship between an increase in ethnic tensions and the worsening of the economy.

Still another cause of prejudice is simple lack of contact with members of other ethnic groups, or at least contact in which people are of equal status. People are naturally more suspicious of what they don't know. A study done in Baltimore, Maryland, recently showed that racially mixed communities had the lowest levels of racial prejudice, and of racially motivated violence. The communities that were predominantly one race were the ones where the most prejudice and the highest levels of racially motivated violence could be found most often.[8]

Another cause of prejudice which few people recognize is lack of education. People who have more education tend to be less prejudiced against members of other ethnic or racial groups. The reasons for this phenomenon are not clear. It may be that reading about people who live in different places or who lived in different times, even if they are of the same race as oneself, helps to make a person generally more tolerant. Whatever the reason, it does seem to be true that education helps to lessen prejudice. In the Baltimore study cited above,

This racially mixed classroom of Native-American and Anglo-American students can be found in Arizona. Studies show that racially mixed communities have the lowest levels of racial prejudice.

the researchers found that degree of education was the factor that, more strongly than all others, influenced the degree of a person's racism.[9]

We have looked in depth at the causes of prejudice because prejudice lies at the root of most problems with ethnic or racial conflict. Some conflicts, however, are caused—or at least made worse—by students' lack of ability to resolve conflicts peacefully. When the only way in which students know how to deal with problems and disagreements is by fighting, conflicts are bound to increase.

By understanding its causes, people can take action to help reduce ethnic conflict. Young people are powerless over some things. Obviously they can't change the political climate of the country, or turn the economy around, or prevent others from being exposed to their parents' prejudice. But they can do something about the contact they have in school with members of other groups. They can do something about the level and content of their education, and about their lack of conflict-resolution skills. In recent years young people *have* done something about these problems. They have developed a wide variety of programs and products aimed at reducing ethnic conflicts. In the next chapter we will look at some of these.

chapter

5

Resolving and
Avoiding Conflicts

Before anything effective can be done in a school to resolve problems with ethnic conflict, an essential first step must be taken. The school must admit a problem exists.

This is not as simple as it may seem. Teachers and especially students may be quick to confirm that there are ethnic tensions at their school. However, many principals have difficulty recognizing or admitting the existence of ethnic or racial tensions in their school. When the United States Education Department surveyed schools about racial tensions, a higher percentage of teachers than principals said they had problems with racial tensions.[1] And unfortunately, little concrete action can be taken to combat such conflicts until those in authority get involved. So admitting that there is a problem in your school is a key step.

One reason schools are sometimes slow to recognize problems with ethnic conflict is that the problems are often hidden. The vast majority of victims of prejudice never report it to anyone in authority. Unless you are consciously looking for signs of tension or conflict, it is easy not to see them. You may need to adopt special strategies in order to see these things. Such strategies can include keeping an eye on interactions between students in the cafeteria or on the playground, asking teachers and counselors to watch for signs of prejudice or tension and to report any they see, noticing whether there are hate crimes in the community (if there are, there will also be conflicts at school), and talking to students about prejudice and conflicts.

Even if evidence of ethnic conflict is obvious and out in the open, many people dismiss it. Principals especially don't want to admit that this exists in their school. They think if they acknowledge it, they are doing a poor job as an administrator. A police sergeant in Passaic County, New Jersey, says that principals often tell him that fights at their schools "aren't a race kind of thing" when in fact they are.[2] A school superintendent in Maryland comments: "People were passing these things off as 'kids will be kids.'" Actually, "these things" were racial or ethnic incidents.[3]

Once you do acknowledge a problem, it is important to follow up with actions that make it clear that prejudice, discrimination, and acts of hate will not be tolerated. "There's no such thing as a non-violent civil rights crime," said Boston police force bias crime specialist William Johnston. "You have to tell kids up front: This won't be tolerated."[4] Here again, the principal, as the school's chief policy maker, plays a key role. Jerome Winegar was principal at South Boston High School, where there were bitter and violent confrontations at the time of the busing controversy. One step he took to confront the problems in his school was to lay down clear rules about behavior that would not be tolerated. "Rule Number 1 is that there's no name-calling here—not even black kids calling each other 'nigger,'" he declared at the time.[5]

But as we all know, policies are just words. They must be followed up by some kind of action. Anti-bias policies are most effective when they are accompanied by dialogue between staff and students, and by action. Teachers and administrators discussing problems of ethnic conflict openly with students can create a helpful atmosphere of commitment and cooperation in solving such problems. Concrete actions also help give weight to what might otherwise be empty words in policy statements.

In 1964 a government agency called the Community Relations Service (CRS) was created as part of the Civil Rights Act of 1964. The agency's purpose was to help communities and individuals to resolve disputes that result from discrimination based on race or ethnic group. In recent years the CRS developed a new program to help secondary schools deal with ethnic and racial tensions. It is aimed specifically at schools whose populations are made up of students from at least three different groups. Named SPIR (Student Problem Identification/Resolution), the program stresses simple recognition and discussion of problems. CRS agents both respond to calls for help and offer their services to schools where the press has reported racial incidents.

When CRS representatives go out to help a school, their first step is to form ethnically homogeneous groups that meet to discuss their problems and concerns and to make lists of suggestions. Representatives from all student groups are included. In the second stage of SPIR, the students come together—this time in mixed groups—to discuss their lists. The principal is then briefed about the outcomes of the discussions and is responsible for conducting follow-up activities.

SPIR has been used in a number of high schools and junior highs, including a rural school with a large population of refugee farm workers, a largely conservative white school which now has minority students bused in, and the Los Angeles schools after the Rodney King riots. The CRS reports considerable success with SPIR, but particularly in cases in which the principal follows up with action.[6] Their results confirm that just confronting the problem of ethnic tensions is in itself helpful—but that follow-up action is also important.

Once schools have admitted that a problem exists and made a clear commitment to doing something about it, there are basically three avenues they can take. Each corresponds to one of the main causes of prejudice that were mentioned in Chapter 4.

Racial and ethnic tensions are highest when groups are isolated from each other. Therefore, one excellent way to reduce tensions is to increase the contact between the differerent racial groups involved. The amount of contact between members of different racial or ethnic groups can be increased in several different ways.

Desegregation. The decades-old tactic of desegregation is the best-known and most radical approach of this kind. Since the 1950s, hundreds of schools across the nation have tried various means of desegregating, both voluntary and forced, in hopes students of different races might learn to live harmoniously with one another. One method is majority-to-minority transfers, which allows or requests that students from minority schools transfer to all-white schools. Another approach involves the use of magnet schools. Special schools with outstanding academic programs allow—and encourage—students from all over a district, of all different backgrounds, to transfer to them. Desegregation can be forced by restructuring a school district. New neighborhood boundaries are drawn which place children of different groups in the same neighborhood school. Elsewhere, mandatory desegregation often relies on pairing, a method in which two schools, one primarily white, the other primarily minority, are "combined." All the younger children from both schools are sent to one location. All the older children from both schools are sent to the other location. Busing is frequently used to achieve these pairings.

The effectiveness of desegregation has been mixed. Some schools report a dramatic increase in racial and ethnic tensions. Schools such as those in Charlotte, North Carolina, offer testimony that desegregation can improve a school's climate tremendously. Boston schools are an example often cited to prove the opposite—that desegregation does not work. The

In this classroom in Fort Meyers, Virginia, in 1964 a black child and a white child face each other on the first class day in history that saw racial integration in some public schools in the South.

results at other schools fall anywhere in between. Studies of desegregation have been inconclusive. Some find that desegregation is effective, others find that it isn't.

Cooperative Learning. A less dramatic method of increasing the contact between students of different groups is the use of cooperative learning. Although less sweeping than desegregation, the opportunities offered by cooperative learning have been proven highly effective.

Let's say a teacher wants to teach his class how to change fractions into percents. He presents the material to the class. Together they work through a couple of problems. Then, instead of simply assigning more problems for homework and announcing a quiz for the next day, he divides the class into four-member teams. Each team includes both boys and girls, members for whom math is easy and those who struggle with it, and members who belong to different racial and ethnic groups. The teacher gives the teams one class period to work together to master the new concepts. At the end of that time, he gives a quiz. The content of the quiz is typical, but the method of grading the papers is not. Each student receives a grade based on how much his or her performance has improved over the last quiz or test he or she took. Then, each team receives a score based on the total of the grades of the four members. In order for their team to do well, members must interact and help one another. Students who can do the work quickly and easily must help the slower ones. Boys and girls, African Americans, Anglo Americans, Hispanic Americans, and others all must work closely together.

Cooperative learning was introduced in the early 1970s as a way to help students learn better. The technique puts students into assigned groups. Each group is given a project, and in order to complete it students must work together. In addition to making learning easier, cooperative learning also helps to break down barriers between racial and ethnic groups and to encourage tolerance. Says cooperative learning pioneer Robert Slavin:

> *Most people use cooperative learning because it's more effective. The nice thing about it is that for free, along the way, you also get improvements in race relations and self-esteem.*[7]

At Germantown Elementary School in Annapolis, Maryland, race relations improved after a cooperative learning program was started. Says Principal Peter Zimmer: "I see a much higher incidence of interracial friendships. Blacks and whites play together more. They sit next to each other at lunch time."[8] In one closely monitored cooperative learning program, students involved in the program were found to have an average of 2.4 friends of another racial group. Students in regular learning environments were reported to have an average of less than one such friend each. A third grade teacher cited dramatic evidence of the effectiveness of cooperative learning. Throughout most of the school year she assigned new learning groups. Each time she regrouped them, she combined students in new ways. For the last month of school, students were allowed to choose their own groups.

They voluntarily organized themselves into racially mixed groups.[9]

Students can increase their everyday interactions with other groups without adopting any one plan or program. They can make efforts to see that extracurricular activities are committed to diversity, that these actively try to recruit students from all groups. They can see that from an early age youngsters of different backgrounds are encouraged to pursue a variety of sports. School athletics can be a terrific opportunity for you to learn to trust and cooperate with others whose background is different from your own. But this can only happen if schools act to prevent kids from choosing their sports based on predictable stereotypes, for example, basketball for black students or tennis for whites.

Education. Education is the second avenue schools can take to promote more harmony between groups. For some years now, it has been popular for schools to celebrate Black History Month or Hispanic Culture Week or Asian Culture Month. Or they hold "cultural fairs" at which students from various ethnic backgrounds offer foods to sample and demonstrate native dances. These small-time efforts, however, are not enough. The kind of program that is truly effective at reducing ethnic conflict must be a far more extensive program of multicultural education. A multicultural education program is one that uses all aspects of the curriculum to promote understanding of the culture of different racial and ethnic groups and to develop in students the values of tolerance and appreciation of diversity. Today, multicultural curriculums often begin with the use of textbooks in all disciplines that are bias-free and that show people of different ethnic backgrounds. Many include workshops for teachers to acquaint them with the cultural backgrounds of their students. Teachers committed to multicultural education give assignments which both help students to become more familiar with their own heritage and help them to learn about cultures other than their own. Students have reported that the adoption of a multicultural approach in their classes—reading selections by writers of different backgrounds in English class, learning about the history of minority groups and the civil rights movement in history class—is the thing they feel has done the most to reduce racial tensions in their school.[10]

One prominent educator, however, offers a note of caution about multicultural education. Diane Ravitch argues that it should be the job of public schools to teach children our country's common culture, more than individual ethnic cultures. If schools neglect to do this, and teach only various ethnic cultures, it can lead to ethnic separateness and increased tensions. A successful multicultural curriculum, she says, must teach the core democratic values that make it possible for people of many different backgrounds to live and work together and make decisions together peaceably. It should teach the history of the institutions that have enabled the United States to build a nation from people of diverse backgrounds. It should teach that ethnic and racial diversity is a source of strength.[11]

Prejudice Reduction Programs. Another effective group of

educational programs is that of prejudice reduction programs. These are programs aimed directly, rather than indirectly, at reducing students' and teachers' prejudices. One of the oldest and most widely used such programs is called "A World of Difference," which was developed by the Anti-Defamation League. The program was started in Boston in 1986, when that city was still struggling with the racial strife that had been stirred up by busing. Today, "A World of Difference" is used in nearly thirty major cities, including New York City.

In one typical "World of Difference" activity, students are asked to identify stereotypes about the different races and genders that show up in comic strips. They examine who is portrayed as hero or as villain, who is portrayed as smart and capable, as dependent on others for help, as brave, as afraid, as successful, as aggressive. After using their findings to create a chart, they discuss the overall images of different groups that emerge, and whether they think the images in comics have influenced their own opinions of these groups. Classes are encouraged to end the activity with a plan to take action. If students are concerned about the way certain groups are portrayed, what are they going to do about it?

Another activity helps to show how stereotypes and prejudice influence people's actions, resulting in discrimination. There are a series of questions about students' own schools: Are there places in your school that are identified as being only for certain groups? Are there certain events that happen in the school that only some groups attend, even though everyone is invited? What happens if a new student enters your school? Is he or she welcomed by everyone?[12]

"World of Difference" programs try to help people examine their stereotypes, expand their awareness of different cultures, combat all forms of bigotry, and explore the value of diversity. They use a variety of methods to accomplish these goals. They help people to explore themselves and identify their own personal prejudices. They teach people to challenge their prejudices and "unlearn" them. They teach problem-solving techniques. They give experiences building teams with others. All these techniques are usually presented to teachers in a twelve-hour training workshop. In the workshop teachers are also given a training guide and instruction in how to use the activities in the guide in their own classroom. To date, over 125,000 teachers have been trained by the staff of "A World of Difference." [13]

Other approaches to prejudice reduction have also been developed. One, "Facing History and Ourselves," emphasizes the upholding of democratic principles and the protection of civil rights. It accomplishes its goals through study of the Holocaust, Nazism, Ku Klux Klan recruitment, and the Rodney King beating.[14] A number of schools have used drama to raise issues of prejudice, differences, and tolerance. The New Jersey Bias Crimes Office started a traveling high school drama group that teaches about prejudice and stereotypes.[15] Brooklyn, New York, has its SPARK players that do theater pieces followed by discussion.[16] Miami has a similar student drama group.[17]

Not long ago at Hillcrest High School in Dallas, Texas, two friends were playing a lunchtime game of basketball. One of the boys was African American, the other Hispanic American. The Hispanic-American boy called his friend a "nigger." Before long, a fight involving over twelve African-American and Hispanic-American students had broken out. The violence soon threatened to spread and involve the whole school.

Instead, the boys involved were asked to sit down with seventeen-year-old student, Sandra Moore, and two other students who assisted her. They talked for four hours. During those four hours, it was discovered that the Hispanic-American students had heard African Americans call each other "nigger" and didn't realize that coming from someone else it was considered an insult. The Hispanic-American students also aired a gripe they had been holding against the African Americans at school. They felt insulted when African-American students made fun of them by imitating their accents.

At the end of the session, the students who had been fighting agreed to leave each other alone and to spread the word that the fight was settled. No immediate new friendships were produced. But violence was prevented, and eventually African-American and Hispanic-American students at Hillcrest began to hang around together again.[18]

The above is an example of peer mediation in action. Of all the approaches to reducing ethnic conflicts in schools, the one that has been cited as most effective most often is that of teaching students problem-solving skills. Programs designed to accomplish this goal go by a number of different names:

"peer mediation," "dispute settlement," "conflict management," and "conflict resolution." Most work in just about the same way.

In one conflict resolution program, students who become peer mediators are specially selected—usually students with proven leadership skills and influence among their fellow students. They then undergo special training in workshops in which they spend hours practicing communication and problem-solving skills. They are taught to be active listeners, to really hear what another person is saying and to empathize with his or her feelings. They are taught to listen to and then articulate the feelings of the person who has just spoken. They learn to see a situation from perspectives other than their own. They learn to refrain from passing judgment, assigning blame, or showing favoritism when they are helping others to resolve a dispute.

When students complete this special training, they are qualified as peer mediators. Disputes between students are referred to them to mediate and help resolve. In some schools, peer mediators can be quickly identified by special T-shirts.

In addition to the special training for peer mediators, most conflict resolution programs include classroom instruction for all students in the basic skills mentioned above. Some include special workshops for parents as well.

Conflict resolution was first introduced in New York City public schools in 1972. Since then it has become a nationwide movement. Today, more than two thousand schools have some form of conflict resolution program. All students in

Chicago's sixty-seven public high schools take courses in dispute resolution. In New Mexico, thirty thousand students in over one hundred schools, including some in remote locations, receive conflict resolution training.[19]

Among those systems where such programs have been adopted, there are many stories of success. School officials in Charlotte, North Carolina, say that between 1989 and 1990, the peer mediation program helped to reduce the number of student assaults by 50 percent. A survey of New York City teachers taken in 1990 found that 71 percent of those surveyed said they noticed less physical violence between students following conflict resolution training. Nearly as many also saw a decrease in name-calling and an increase in students' willingness to cooperate with each other.[20]

Anti-discrimination policies, cooperative learning, multicultural education, prejudice reduction programs, peer mediation—surely with so many dynamic new initiatives being taken, there must be hope for the problem of ethnic conflicts in our schools. If you are interested in starting one of these programs in your school, talk to a teacher or principal. It *can* be done.

6

No More Conflict— Is It Possible?

On a Thursday afternoon, after they had already put in a full day of teaching, about fifteen teachers at Carol City Middle School in Miami, Florida, squeezed themselves into the desks in one of the school's classrooms. Among the many examples of student work on the room's cheerful and busy walls hung a poster, "Rules for Fighting Fair." The teachers were about one-third Anglo American, two-thirds minority (some of these Hispanic Americans, but most African Americans). Although a few of the Anglo-American teachers did sit together, as did a few of the African-American teachers, everyone in the room joined in good-natured bantering as they waited for the workshop to begin. A number of students from the school's nearly all African-American student body poked their heads in, looking for this or that teacher for various after-school activities.

At 2:15 P.M. a young black man and a middle-aged white woman entered, briefcase and easel in hand. They were John

Caudle and Norma Whittum, North Miami's Region Two Intergroup Relations Team. Together the two introduced the Carol City teachers to the concept of conflict resolution. By having them work in groups on a hypothetical problem facing a faculty committee, they helped the teachers to learn about the various "styles of conflict resolution" different people use to tackle problems. The teachers were presented with a make-believe problem: a school has been given a large grant of money, and a decision must be made today as to how the money will be spent, or the grant will go to another school. The presidents of various student groups, such as the band, the science club, and the debate team, must meet and together reach a decision as to who will get the money. Different teachers were assigned the roles of the various club presidents and, at the same time, secretly assigned a "style" of conflict resolution. (Examples of these include "the sheep," who goes along with what others want to do, "the ostrich," who tries to avoid conflict, and "the shark," who uses aggressive tactics to get things to go his way.) At the end everyone was to guess who had been the sheep, the ostrich, and so on. At the end of the workshop Norma Whittum discussed the pros and cons of the different approaches to handling conflict. She then explained that those who attended next time would get to practice mediating a dispute between two students.

Yes, there would be a "next time." This was the third in a series of workshops being presented at Carol City Middle School as part of Miami's PROUD (Peacefully Resolving Our Unsettled Differences), a conflict mediation and violence reduction program. The last one had taken place not long before, at 7:30 A.M. For this workshop, students' parents had been invited. One of the teachers had brought in photographs for the others to see. These showed tables full of men and women, neatly dressed and obviously ready to leave for work, yet still smiling and attentive. They had come out early—in large numbers—to learn how they could intervene more effectively when their children got into disputes outside of school.

What is happening at Carol City Middle School is typical of Dade County, Florida's huge school system. Twenty-five years ago this system, which runs the public schools in Miami and surrounding communities, was a typical segregated southern school system. There were separate schools for blacks and whites. Today, the system is largely integrated, but some schools still bear signs of the segregated past. Although the faculty at Carol City is mixed, for example, its student body is still basically all-black. Yet Carol City is typical in its involvement in new efforts to confront and resolve problems of ethnic and racial tensions in Miami's ethnically diverse inner-city schools.

The first efforts to confront the issues of prejudice and ethnic tension in Miami schools were made under court order. In the 1970s, Judge Atkins directed Miami to use whatever methods were required, including forced busing, to achieve desegregation in its schools "with all deliberate speed." He also ordered that the faculty at each school be integrated: at senior highs, between 12 and 28 percent black, at middle schools between 21 and 43 percent black, and at elementary

At Carol City Middle School in Dade County Florida, parents eagerly attended the early morning meetings as part of the school's conflict management program. They were there to learn how to more effectively intervene when their children got into disputes outside of school.

schools between 24 and 30 percent black. The schools responded with a variety of measures. They used pairing. A black school and a white school were paired and the younger children from both schools were put together in one building. The older children from the two schools were put together in another. They created magnet schools, schools that had special programs or a special theme, to attract students of all races from across the city. They also used "minority to majority transfer," or busing of black children into formerly all-white schools in another neighborhood. The teachers with the least seniority were required to transfer to other schools in order to achieve the required ratios.

The first years of desegregation created a great deal of new tensions in the schools. Many parents were opposed to children being bused. Many teachers resented being forced to transfer to new schools. Formerly all-black schools felt especially hard hit. Since so many of their teachers were required to move in order to create a faculty that was only 20 or 30 percent black, they lost a great many experienced teachers. Students, teachers, and parents often had difficulty getting used to dealing with people whose customs were very different from their own. Incidents of racial violence were common. There were riots that often involved dozens of students.

Today, most people point to a number of good results that have come of the process, such as people having fewer stereotypes about members of different races. Said one woman who had been a teacher at the time, "One of the biggest benefits was mixing us all up." There are still people who wish desegregation had never happened. A few old tensions and resentments remain. One school, for example, recently neglected to do anything to celebrate Black History Month.

But by far the largest problem now confronting Miami's schools is the city's new ethnic diversity. According to recent statistics, Miami schools are 34 percent black, 48 percent Hispanic-American, 17 percent white, and 1 percent Asian-American, Native American, and other. But this standard breakdown doesn't begin to show the many groups in the county's system. Miami has been the destination for recent immigrants from dozens of different nations all over the world. Students in the city's schools come from 147 different countries. Now, black students are not all African Americans. Some are Haitians, some are Jamaicans, some are Africans, and some are from Latin America. Hispanic-American students are not all Cuban. They may come from any one of many different islands or Central or South American countries. Even the white student population is diverse. It includes, for example, a growing number of Russian immigrants.

The new diversity has created many new problems and tensions. Many new immigrants do not speak English. Misunderstandings arise when members of one group find the cultural practices of another group "weird." Haitian children, for example, get teased because their religion forbids them to celebrate Halloween.

Yet the Miami schools have confronted these new problems and tensions head-on. There are a host of new policies and programs designed to directly address the issues that have come with the new ethnic diversity.

The first step that was taken was in 1989, when improvement of intergroup relations was made an official system-wide goal. This decision led, in 1990, to the establishment of a new Division of Multicultural Programs. The official goal of the new division was "to ensure that each child [be] given the opportunity to develop pride in his/her ethnicity and to gain understanding, respect, and an appreciation of the ethnicity of others." The responsibilities of the division were to go far beyond simply recognizing special ethnic holidays or organizing ethnic festivals and food fairs. They were to include revising the curriculum in all subject areas to give it a multicultural focus, providing training for administrators and teachers, and working with community groups to promote multicultural education programs. Special multicultural staff was assigned in each region to develop the new programs.

The new division decided that the most pressing need in the system was for a conflict management program. In 1991 Project PROUD was introduced. The program was to be put into effect in phases. During the first phase, one administrator, one teacher, and one student from each school were trained in conflict management/peer mediation and received the materials needed to start up a student peer mediation program in their school. During the second phase, two teachers from each school were trained to help their fellow teachers begin using new textbooks. These would teach students in every classroom better, nonviolent ways to resolve their own

Mediation in Action is a program in Miami that helps prepare student peer mediators to deal with issues that come up in their schools. It teaches nonviolent ways to resolve conflicts and to mediate disputes.

conflicts and, eventually, mediate others' disputes. Techniques such as telling the truth, listening to others without interrupting, showing respect for others' points of view (by avoiding name-calling, blaming, and bringing up the past), and taking responsibility for carrying out any agreement reached are among those stressed.

There was also a parent education component to the PROUD program, called "Fighting Fair for Families." A core group of twelve parents was trained in family-oriented conflict resolution and mediation skills. This core group then went out and trained hundreds more, in breakfast workshops such as the one held at Carol City. The materials for the program were produced by the Peace Education Foundation, a Miami-based organization with a national reputation for their work. The parent materials are available in Spanish and Haitian Creole as well as English.

Enthusiasm for PROUD has grown steadily among staff and students alike. In December of 1993, twenty-six hundred North Miami Beach high school students held an anti-violence rally. In the spring of 1994, several hundred students from all over the county who had actually done mediation in their schools attended a peace education conference. There they shared their experience and sharpened their skills. The school administration now publishes a newsletter solely devoted to mediation.

The peer mediation program also seems to be part of a larger movement among students to take more responsibility for helping one another. Students at a number of high schools have sent teams of students trained in mediation out to junior high schools and elementary schools to help students there solve problems. A group of students from Miami Beach sponsors "immigration workshops" for students in Little Haiti. They travel into the inner city at night to meet with the students they help. They work with the Haitian students to help them resolve the many different problems people new to this country experience.

Multicultural specialists, known as Intergroup Relations teams, have done much more than organize and coordinate PROUD, however. They have worked to make multicultural texts available to teachers in all subjects, at all grade levels. They have overseen the establishment of programs designed to raise the cultural awareness and ethnic pride of specific groups. One such program is AESOP (Afrocentric Enhancement and Self-Esteem Opportunity Program), designed for African Americans. The teams have helped students produce skits and plays that dramatize the need for respecting those who are different from themselves. These plays have been taken into the elementary and junior high schools. The teams have also continuously sponsored workshops and training sessions for teachers and students.

The Miami Beach school system's commitment to improving relations between ethnic and racial groups can also be seen now in its official policies. Their code of ethics requires that an educator "shall not harass or discriminate against any student on the basis of race, color, religion, sex, age, national or ethnic origin, political beliefs, marital status, handicapping condition, sexual orientation, or social and family background and shall make reasonable effort to assure that each student is protected from harassment or discrimination."

The Code of Student Conduct for Secondary Students in Dade County Schools defines as Group II Violations (violations punishable by suspension, among other options) "any slurs, innuendos, or other verbal or physical conduct reflecting on an individual's gender, race, color, religion, ethnic or national origin, age, sexual orientation, social and family background, linguistic preference, or disability, which has the purpose or effect of creating an intimidating, hostile, or offensive educational environment."

The system has made a special effort to establish policies that ensure mixing between different groups. It recently ruled, for example, that a school's "Brain Bowl" team had to have the same ethnic/racial mix as the school as a whole did. (In "Brain Bowl" tournaments, students compete to see who can correctly answer questions in various subject areas the fastest.)

What have been the results of all these new programs, all this new activity? How effective have PROUD, and the tireless efforts of the Intergroup Relations Teams actually been? The programs are all too new for formal evaluations to have been completed yet. Extensive data is being gathered on such things as the number, type, and locations of conflicts reported, the incidents of student mediation, and students' and teachers' assessments of the effectiveness of PROUD training and classroom instruction. But the evaluation has yet to be finalized.

Informal observations yield mixed reactions. According to one Intergroup Relations Team, the number of incidents of racial or ethnic hostility is definitely down from what it was in the years immediately following desegregation. There is much less name-calling, less racially motivated graffiti, fewer large fights and riots. The majority of students today have mixed groups of friends—a rare phenomenon in years past.

Some students still make charges of ethnic or racial discrimination. Some students and teachers still tend to segregate themselves by ethnic or racial group in the cafeteria and at school social functions. About 10 percent of Miami's schools have all African-American students. These, however, are the remains of problems that were once much more severe.

Gangs. One problem has actually been getting worse, despite the new programs and efforts. This is the problem of gangs and gang-related violence. Each district in the Miami system employs one or more "gang specialists," who are kept very busy. A gang specialist in one region estimates that in her area, probably half the students of middle school age are gang members. Increasingly, girls are also joining gangs.

The gangs are sometimes ethnically mixed, but often their members are from a single ethnic group, such as American blacks, black Puerto Ricans, or Haitian blacks. Clashes between gangs frequently pit these various groups of blacks against one another. The gang conflicts that take place after school make for an increase in ethnic and racial tensions during school as well. The rise in gang membership has also brought an increase in schoolyard fights and acts of violence that are racially or ethnically motivated. Some schools report one or two such incidents a week. And now, three out of five such fights involve the use of guns or other weapons. There has also been a tremendous amount of gang-related graffiti.

The problem of gangs has proved a particularly difficult one to crack. Students join gangs for a variety of reasons. Some of these reasons are economic. Times have been harder recently, and gangs make money—by stealing and selling, or by drug sales. The most common reason for joining a gang, however, is a need to feel a sense of belonging. Parents often have to work two to three jobs, and, when they finally do come home, are too tired to want to deal with their children. Gangs provide the missing sense of family. These deeper societal problems go beyond what schools are able to deal with. Added to that is the tremendous difficulty of getting a young person out of a gang once he or she has joined. Gang specialists feel they have done well if they manage to get a half a dozen kids out of gangs in a year.

The Miami schools should be applauded for their efforts. More than many inner-city systems, they have been willing to acknowledge and confront the difficult problem of ethnic tension. They have shown daring, creativity, and commitment in their efforts to find ways to tackle the problem. It may just be that the problem of ethnic and racial tensions has causes too deeply rooted in the structure of our society to be solved in a few short years by even the most dedicated school staff.

Newton, Massachusetts, is as different a community from Miami, Florida, as can be imagined. A relatively affluent

When a gang member is killed by someone in another gang, a member of the dead person's gang writes or creates his specific tag followed by "RIP" to indicate that another gang member killed him.

suburb of Boston, it boasts graciously tree-lined streets and well-kept older homes ranging from tidy to stately. It is a community that takes a great deal of pride in its schools. Newton North High School, one of the town's two public high schools, is an impressive work of modern architecture that an observer would be surprised to learn is twenty-five years old. Its playful, unusual angles and spaces are the work of someone who clearly had progressive, liberal ideas about education and the environment for it.

Progressive, liberal thinking is something of a tradition in Newton. It has a long and proud history. In the years before the Civil War, Newton was the last stop on the Underground Railroad, the network of people opposed to slavery who helped smuggle slaves out of the South, to the North and freedom. In fact, a percentage of the town's black population today is still made up of descendants of the Africans who arrived in Newton in the 1850s in search of their freedom.

In 1974, the Supreme Court of the United States ruled that suburbs could not be required to be involved in busing plans with a neighboring large city. (Officials in the Detroit area had tried to correct the racial imbalance in their inner-city schools by requiring that black inner-city students be bused out to largely white schools in the surrounding suburbs. The Supreme Court ruled the plan unconstitutional.)

Even though it was not required, Newton voluntarily decided in 1971 to begin busing in black students from inner-city Boston. The citizens hoped the busing, known as the Metco Program, would give some inner-city young people educational opportunities they would otherwise never have. They also thought it would be a good thing for Newton students if there were more of a racial balance in the school. (Before the busing began only about twenty-five out of Newton North High's three thousand students were black.) A special counselor was hired whose sole job was seeing to the needs of the students who were being bused. She worked tirelessly to help all the school's black students raise their level of academic achievement and change their attitudes about themselves and what they were capable of.

In 1986 a student organization called Ethos for Equality was formed. The purpose of the group was to help students to face their prejudices and to try to change them. The organization soon took on an additional function. It helped students to bring issues of racism and discrimination to the attention of the administration.

It certainly seemed that Newton North, with its praiseworthy efforts to help inner-city blacks and its liberal attitudes of concern about prejudice and racial inequality, was a most unlikely candidate for racial violence.

On Friday, November 15, 1991, a student dropped a pen down a stairwell and it hit a white student. Four black ninth graders were walking by at the time. The student who had been hit accused one of the four, Paris Wilkey, of having dropped it. Within minutes, a group of four white boys were calling Paris and his friends "nigger" and other racial slurs and obscenities. Paris was on the football team and knew that if he got into a fight he would not be allowed to play, so he and his friends refused to take up the white students' challenge. But they quickly ran to find friends who would be willing to come back and confront the white students.

Within minutes the school had mass chaos on its hands. Both whites and blacks rallied to the defense of their friends. The white students continued to shout racial slurs. Black girls were called bitches. One white boy spit at a black girl. Even after a teacher managed to pin him against the wall, he continued spitting and biting. A black girl got hysterical and began swinging a crutch wildly at anyone white who came near her. The teachers and administration attempted to stop the fighting by bringing all the black students into an empty classroom. But the students, angry at being penned, as they saw it, like a bunch of animals when they had been the victims of abuse, soon broke out. There were loud shouting matches between teachers and young people. It was a miracle no one was physically hurt.

The incident was only ended when the principal ordered all students to their homerooms, summoned the Metco buses, and called for an early dismissal. The end of the school day that Friday was more a beginning than an ending. It was the beginning of Newton North's confrontation with some bitter truths about the relations between the different racial and ethnic groups there.

Paris Wilkey has been bused from his inner-city Boston home to outlying schools since first grade. He recalls that tensions between blacks and whites had existed since he was in junior high. There had been incidents of racially based fights at Newton North in the years prior to the November 15 outbreak. The tensions that resulted from these incidents were brought under control, but not always resolved.

After the Friday eruption, the school could no longer ignore the issue. The school's first efforts were aimed at the immediate goal of restoring order and at least a minimally acceptable level of trust among students. Teachers tried to contact the family of every black student and reassure them that their children would not be harmed or unfairly treated. They met all weekend long and invited students and parents, both black and white, to meet with them. For the reopening of school on Monday an all-school assembly was planned at which students, the principal, and community leaders would speak about what happened.

When Monday came, tensions were still sky-high. Some students were still so shaken that they were crying. Still, everyone filed into the gym for the school's first all-school assembly ever. In addition to the principal and the mayor, a rabbi, a minister from a local black church, and three students spoke. The captain of the football team, David Lewis, a young white man named Michael Gavin, and a black girl, Tamika Taylor, all spoke. David, who is black, spoke about how you didn't need to like another kid, but how you did have to respect him. He made a plea for everyone to put the violence and hatred of the incident behind him or her. Tamika talked about the hurt that racial slurs inflict.

In the immediate aftermath of November 15, there were special homeroom sessions to give students a chance to talk about what had happened and to express their feelings. The staff made a point of responding to every single racial incident immediately, no matter how minor. Every piece of graffiti was removed as soon as it was spotted. It seemed things were returning to some kind of normalcy.

The following year was the year in which Los Angeles police officers were tried and acquitted of unjustly beating Rodney King. It was at this time that staff members began to notice outbreaks of swastika graffiti. Finally a group of students approached a member of the administration and said that washing walls was just not enough. More had to be done.

Students eventually convinced James Marini, the principal, that another all-school assembly was needed. This time the keynote speaker was the regional director of the Anti-Defamation League, Leonard Zakim. Mr. Zakim began by calling for eighty-one seconds of silence. That was how long, he said, Rodney King had been beaten. The silence that flooded that gym for those eighty-one seconds seemed eternal.

That assembly proved a turning point for Newton North. Although it had featured an adult speaker, the assembly itself was largely the product of student initiative. This fact had wide-reaching effects. First, it showed that students can make a difference, that students can take actions which might actually produce change. Second, it woke teachers and administrators up to the fact that many students don't feel enough is being done about the problems of ethnic and racial tension.

The school year 1992–1993 was a landmark in the history of racial relations at Newton North. Both students and staff made tremendous efforts to confront and improve the situation. The day riots broke out in Los Angeles after the Rodney King verdict, Newton North's Metco students held a daylong speak-in on the school library steps. Not long after, a black student and a white student formed an organization called "Common Ground" that visited various churches and synagogues and attempted to understand what people of different backgrounds had in common.

Another small group of students—one black and two Jewish—formed an organization called the Human Rights Coalition. The goal of the Coalition was to coordinate the efforts of the school's various human rights and cultural organizations in order to make them more effective. It also established a subcommittee, the "Committee for Multicultural Curriculum," that has written special academic units, such as one on the Japanese internment during World War II, that have a multicultural focus.

In its first year, the Coalition wrote and produced an award-winning series of playlets that focused on situations in which people had to confront issues of race and prejudice. One playlet was about the conflicts a girl of mixed (black-white) parents faced. Another was about a black boy and a white boy who had been close friends in grade school but found themselves being separated by racial pressures when they reached high school. The third was about the struggles of a "hip" liberal family whose teenage son had turned out to be very conservative. The production was honored by the mayor and the local Anti-Defamation League.

Commitment to dealing with problems of ethnic and racial tension also increased dramatically. The principal adopted a policy of addressing such problems immediately and forthrightly. A special position was created, called "Coordinator of Intercultural Affairs." The man who filled it, Scott Guild, was to concern himself not just with black-white relations, but with tensions within the school's black community (between Newton blacks and Metco blacks), and with the interests of the school's other growing ethnic communities—Asians, Russian immigrants, and others.

Mr. Guild began immediately to pump new energy into programs aimed at improving relations among all the school's different ethnic groups. He has seen to it that the school maintains ongoing commitments to programs that have proven helpful in reducing tensions and helping students to resolve intergroup (and other) problems. These include a peer mediation program called PAWS ("positive agreement works") which conducts about forty mediations a year, annual leadership retreats for "influential" students which teach leadership and group-building skills and try to foster a human rights awareness, and regularly scheduled forums at which students and teachers can discuss sensitive issues together. He also conducts workshops for teachers, provides faculty support and advice for the Human Rights Coalition, and serves as a liaison with community human rights groups in which Newton North students are involved.

How much progress has all this activity produced since the November 15, 1991, incident? Has there been any decrease in ethnic and racial tensions? Assistant Principal Gail Stein, who has been closely involved with Newton North's minority students for years, is optimistic. She points out that there is much more mingling between black and white students and between Newton blacks and Metco blacks. Some people, she says, recently thought they were in the wrong place when they walked into a school entertainment program combining Irish and gospel music and saw so many blacks in the audience. And she cites as an example the young black girl who spoke at the all-school assembly held the Monday after the November 1991 incident. As a freshman, Tamika Taylor would have nothing to do with whites. When she graduated she had many white friends.

However, both the principal, James Marini, and Intercultural Affairs Coordinator Scott Guild are guarded. Mr. Marini believes the level of racial harmony hasn't changed much. Says Scott Guild, "Racism is not a problem you solve; it has ebbs and flows. It's never going to be done away with."

Student opinion runs along similar lines. Black students who were at Newton North at the time of the November 15, 1991, incident say they think there are still tensions. Blacks and whites still tend to segregate themselves in the cafeteria. "Things never got back to normal," says Paris Wilkey. Those students who do find some truth in Mrs. Stein's view don't credit any of the many faculty- or student-initiated special programs with the progress. Instead, they point to the simple fact that blacks are getting more involved in extracurricular

Peer mediators like the ones shown in this picture try to work out sensitive issues in their school, in nonviolent ways.

activities. This gives them a chance to get to know more white students.

An inner-city, only recently desegregated school system in the deep South, and a "model" school in a suburb known for its liberal attitudes and an overt commitment to racial equality: in both we have seen deep-seated problems of racial and ethnic conflict. In both cases, the school community has squarely acknowledged the problems and gone on to make heroic efforts to conquer them—far more than has been done in the vast majority of American communities. Yet in both cases only modest progress can be claimed. Clearly we must conclude that the ethnic conflict in our schools is among this country's most stubborn problems.

Yet this is not cause for despair. For the two case studies described in this chapter also show that with sufficient dedication and effort, progress *is* possible. And if every generation of students could make as much progress in its six or seven years of middle school and high school as has been made in the past few years in Miami and Newton, the twenty-first century could see the end of ethnic tensions in our schools. So let the examples of these two schools serve as sources of inspiration to you rather than discouragement.

Chapter Notes

Chapter 1

This story is based on reporting in the *San Jose Mercury News,* (August 21, 1990), p. 1B.

Chapter 2

1. Patricia and Frederick McKissack, *Taking a Stand Against Racism and Racial Discrimination* (New York: Franklin Watts, 1990), p. 14.

2. Sarah Evelyn Wright, "Teaching Strategies Used with Non-European Immigrant Students in New York City High Schools," Dissertation, Teachers College, 1988, p. 45.

3. Ibid., p. 41.

4. Diane Ravitch, *The Great School Wars: New York City 1805–1973—A History of the Public Schools as Battlefield of Social Change* (New York: Basic Books, 1974), p. 168.

5. Ibid., pp. 170–171.

6. Ibid., pp. 168–169.

7. Ibid., p. 244.

8. Ibid., p. 177.

9. Ibid.

10. Ibid., p. 176.

11. Ibid.

12. Ibid., p. 244.

13. Jon Hillson, *The Battle of Boston* (New York: Pathfinder, 1977), p. 42.

14. Ibid., p. 43.

15. Emma Gelders Sterne, *They Took Their Stand* (New York: Crowell-Collier Press, 1968), p. 197.

16. "Civil Rights U.S.A.: Public Schools, Southern States, 1962," Staff Reports Submitted to the U.S. Commission on Civil Rights, p. 33.

17. Howard Maniloff, "Community Attitudes Toward a Desegregated School System: A Study of Charlotte, North Carolina," Dissertation, Teachers College, 1979, p. 42.

18. Ibid., p. 46.

19. Ibid.

20. Ibid., p. 49.

21. Ibid., p. 52.

22. Hillson, p. 45.

23. Ibid.

24. Ibid., p. 23.

25. Ibid., p. 91.

26. Ibid., p. 250.

27. Maniloff, p. 80.

28. Ibid.

29. Ibid., p. 28.

30. Robert A. Pratt: *The Color of Their Skin: Education and Race in Richmond, Virginia 1954–1989* (Charlottesville, Va.: University Press of Virginia, 1992), p. 106.

31. Ibid., pp. 89–91.

Chapter 3

1. John O'Neil, "A New Generation Confronts Racism," *Educational Leadership*, Vol. 50, (May 1993), p. 60.

2. Michael Meek, "The Peacekeepers: Students Use Mediation Skills to Resolve Conflicts," *Teaching Tolerance*, Vol. 1 (Fall 1992), p. 48.

3. Interview with Wilma Austin, School Social Worker, Jacksonville, Florida, Public Schools. March, 1994.

4. O'Neil, p. 60.

5. Donna Harrington-Lueker, "Teaching Tolerance," *Executive Educator*, Vol. 15 (May 1993), p. 15.

6. Harold Cruse, cited in Robert P. Formisano, *Boston Against Busing* (Chapel Hill, N.C.: University of North Carolina Press, 1991), p. 18.

7. Patricia and Frederick McKissack, *Taking a Stand Against Racism and Racial Discrimination* (New York: Franklin Watts, 1990), p. 75.

8. Dionne J. Jones and Monica L. Jackson, "Racism and Interracial Violence: A Clear and Present Danger," *Urban League Review*, Vol. 15 (Summer 1991), p. 9.

9. O'Neil, p. 60.

10. Meek, pp. 48–52.

11. Ibid.

12. Harrington-Lueker, p. 15.

13. Meek, p. 49.

14. Del Stover, "Racism Redux," *Executive Educator*, Vol. 15 (Feb. 1993), p. 35.

15. Harrington-Lueker, p. 15.

16. O'Neil, p. 61.

17. Ibid.

18. Meek, p. 48.

19. Ibid.

20. James W. Boothe, T. Michael Flick, et al., "The Violence at Your Door," *Executive Educator*, Vol. 15 (Feb. 1993), p. 20.

21. Debra Ladestro, "Teaching Tolerance," *Teachers Magazine*, Vol. 2 (Feb. 1991), p. 26.

22. Ibid.

23. Ibid.

24. Dionne J. Jones, "The College Campus as a Microcosm of U.S. Society: The Issue of Racially Motivated Violence," *Urban League Review*, Vol. 13 (Summer–Winter 1989–1990), p. 132.

25. Meek, p. 48.

26. Stover, p. 35.

27. Ibid.

28. Ibid.

29. Jones, p. 133.

30. Pat Ordovensky, "Facing Up to Violence," *Executive Educator*, Vol. 15 (Feb. 1993), p. 23.

31. Boothe, Flick, et al., p. 19.

32. McKissack, p. 21.

33. Interview with Connie Cuddle, Director of Student Activities, Brooklyn, New York, Crown Heights District, March 1994.

34. Interview with Norma Whittum, Intergroup Relations Team, Dade County, Florida, Schools, Region II, March 1994.

35. Sheldon S. Varney and Kenneth Cushner, "Understanding Cultural Diversity Can Improve Intercultural Interactions," *NASSP Bulletin*, Vol. 40 (Oct. 1990), p. 89.

36. Interview with Gail Stein, Asst. Principal, Newton North High School, Newton, Mass., March 1994.

37. G. Genevieve Patthey-Chavez, "High School As an Arena for Cultural Conflict and Acculturation for Latino Angelinos," *Anthropology and Education Quarterly*, Vol. 24 (March 1993), p. 33.

38. Ibid.

39. Interview with Carol Conger, Superintendent of Schools, Chatham, New Jersey, March 1994.

40. Interview with Alberta Flannery, Director of Native American Studies Dept. for Tucson, Arizona, Unified School District, March 1994.

41. Ibid.

42. Ibid.

43. *Encyclopedia of Educational Research* (1992).

44. Ibid.

45. David Brand, "The New Whiz Kids," *Time,* as abridged in Linda Schinke-llano, ed., *We the People* (Lincolnwood, Ill.: National Textbook Company, 1992), p. 40.

46. Ibid.

47. Ibid.

Chapter 4

1. John O'Neil, "A New Generation Confronts Racism," *Educational Leadership,* Vol. 50 (May 1993), p. 67.

2. Patricia and Frederick, *Taking a Stand Against Racism and Racial Discrimination* (New York: Franklin Watts, 1990), pp. 13–14.

3. Dionne J. Jones and Monica L. Jackson, "Racism and Interracial Violence: A Clear and Present Danger," *Urban League Review,* Vol. 15 (Summer 1991), p. 10.

4. McKissack, p. 15.

5. Interview with Alberta Flannery, director of Native American Studies Dept. for Tucson, Arizona, Unified School District, March 1994.

6. Jones and Jackson, p. 136.

7. Ibid.

8. Ibid., pp. 17–18.

9. Ibid., p. 19.

Chapter 5

1. Pat Ordovensky, "Facing Up to Violence," *Executive Educator,* Vol. 15 (Feb. 1993), p. 22.

2. Donna Harrington-Lueker, "Teaching Tolerance," *Executive Educator,* Vol. 15 (May 1993), p. 19.

3. Ibid.

4. Ibid., p. 16.

5. Ibid.

6. Julian Klugman and Barbara Greenberg, "Programs Help Identify, Resolve Problems in Multicultural High Schools," *NASSP Bulletin*, Vol. 75 (Dec. 1991), p. 98.

7. Debra Ladestro, "Teaching Tolerance," *Teachers Magazine*, Vol. 2 (Feb. 1991), p. 26.

8. Ibid.

9. Ibid., p. 27.

10. Interview with students at North Newton High School, Newton, Massachusetts, March 1994.

11. Diane Ravitch, "A Culture in Common," *Educational Leadership*, Vol. 49 (Dec.–Jan. 1991), pp. 8–10.

12. Florida Regional Office of the Anti-Defamation League, "A World of Difference" newspaper supplement for secondary students developed for the Connecticut Newspaper in Education Council, 1993.

13. Interview with Marji Lipshez, Anti-Defamation League, New Haven, Conn., January 1994.

14. Harrington-Lueker, p. 18.

15. Ibid., p. 19.

16. Interview with Connie Cuddle, Director of Student Activities, Crown Heights District, Brooklyn, New York, Public Schools, March 1994.

17. Interview with Norma Whittum, Intergroup Relations Team, Dade County, Florida, Public Schools, Region II, March 1994.

18. Michael Meek, "The Peacekeepers: Students Use Meditation Skills to Resolve Conflicts," *Teaching Tolerance*, Vol. 1 (Fall 1992), p. 46.

19. Ibid., p. 48.

20. Ibid., pp. 50–51.

Chapter 6

Material in this chapter is based on March 1994 interviews with various people in Region II of the Dade County, Florida, Public Schools, especially the Intergroups Relations Team of Norma Whittum and John Caudle, and a number of people—administrators, teachers, students—at Newton North High School, Newton, Massachusetts.

Glossary

busing–Transporting students by bus in order to desegregate schools.

conflict resolution program–A program designed to help students resolve conflicts among themselves constructively, without resorting to violence.

cooperative learning–A teaching method which has students of varying ability levels and backgrounds work together and help each other to learn.

desegregation–A policy of eliminating segregation.

ethnic group–A group whose members are bound together by a shared history, culture, nationality, or religion.

graffiti–Drawings or writings on a wall or other surface.

hate crime–A crime that is motivated by prejudice against members of a particular racial, ethnic, or religious group.

multicultural education–An educational program that stresses respect for people's different cultures.

peer mediation–A technique of using specially trained students to help other students resolve their conflicts constructively.

prejudice–A judgment based on previous decisions formed before the facts were known.

racial group–A group of people who share certain physical traits and often share a common history and culture as well.

segregation–Separation of people on the basis of their race or ethnic group.

white flight–The phenomenon of white students leaving public schools in large numbers when a policy of desegregation is announced.

Further Reading

Barden, Renardo. *Gangs.* (Vero Beach, FL: Rourke Corporation, 1990).

Dudley, William and Cozie. Charles. *Racism in America: Opposing Viewpoints.* (San Diego, Greenhaven Press, 1991).

Katz, William L. *Minorities Today.* (Raintree Steck-Vaughn, 1992).

Kronenwetter, Michael. *Prejudice in America: Causes and Cures* (New York: Franklin Watts, 1993).

Langone, John. *Spreading Poison: A Book About Racism and Prejudice.* (New York: Little, Brown, 1993).

McKissack, Patricia and Fredrick. *Taking a Stand Against Racism and Racial Discrimination.* (New York: Franklin Watts, 1990).

Meier, Gisela. *Minorities.* (Vero Beach, FL: Rourke Corporation, 1991).

Osborn, Kevin. *Everything You Need to Know about Bias Incidents.* (New York: Rosen Group, 1993).

Ryan, Elizabeth A. *Straight Talk About Prejudice.* (New York: Facts on File, 1992).

Index